GUIDED**PRACTICE** **ROUTINES**FOR**GUITAR**

INTERMEDIATE LEVEL

Practice with 125 Guided Exercises in this Comprehensive 10-Week Guitar Course

LEVI**CLAY**

FUNDAMENTAL**CHANGES**

Guided Practice Routines For Guitar – Intermediate Level

Practice with 125 Guided Exercises in this Comprehensive 10-Week Guitar Course

ISBN: 978-1-78933-418-0

Published by **www.fundamental-changes.com**

Copyright © 2023 Levi Clay

Edited by Tim Pettingale

www.fundamental-changes.com

Over 12,000 fans on Facebook: **FundamentalChangesInGuitar**

Instagram: **FundamentalChanges**

For over 350 Free Guitar Lessons with Videos Check Out

www.fundamental-changes.com

Cover Image Copyright: Shutterstock

Contents

Introduction

Music provides us with one of the world's great personal struggles. Like learning to paint, swim, cook or dance, it requires repetition and practice to achieve the goals we set for ourselves. There's nothing more frustrating than the feeling that we're just spinning our wheels and never getting anywhere. Practice is always the way out of that.

Music is complicated because it's both a physical act (like swimming) and a form of expression (like painting). It has the additional baggage of being like a language, with its own vocabulary and grammar. But unlike learning French or German, the words are much more abstract. They have meaning, but the meaning is found in how they make us feel.

Achieving mastery of something so complicated is a pipe dream for most. I've been playing guitar for 20 years and I don't ever expect to reach the level of *pure mastery*. But I'm going to keep working at it, because if can't achieve absolute mastery, I can hope for a degree of fluency. Fluency means being able to express oneself with creative, musical ideas, and possessing the technique necessary to play them. The aim of this series is to help you become fluent on your instrument.

I've been doing weekly guided practice routines with my student base for over a year now. It was something I started doing after my piano teacher did it with me and I saw rapid growth in my playing. After seeing immediate results in the playing of my guitar students, it felt like it was time to bring these practice routines to a wider audience. They will give your practice sessions a sense of organisation, so that you know what your goals are before you sit down to play.

This is book two in the series. Book one covered foundational skills. It's not essential for you to have read the first book, but in this volume, it's assumed you have a good level of core skills and theoretical knowledge. The drills in the first book should be relatively easy to you and under your fingers already. This book will build on the foundations laid in the previous volume and equip you with the skills you need to move on to a more advanced level.

Remember, when we learn something in music, we need it to become unconscious. We don't practice until we get it right, we practice until we can't get it wrong. I cannot stress this enough. If you're coming to this volume from book one, make sure you have that material down. If there are any elements of the foundational material you're unsure of, don't move forward until you've sorted them. A house built on rock-solid foundations will stand the test of time. It's much easier to build a house on concrete than jelly! You're only cheating yourself if you're not adequately prepared.

If you've come to this book fresh, without working through book one, Chapter One provides a refresher course of some of the essential techniques it covered. It will help make sure you know that stuff well enough to keep going.

Take each of these routines and use the audio to practice along with me every day. After a week, if you're ready to move on to the next routine, do it. If you need another week, take it.

Above all, work hard and have fun.

Levi.

Get the Audio

The audio files for this book are available to download for free from **www.fundamental-changes.com.** The link is in the top right-hand corner. Click on the "Guitar" link then simply select this book title from the drop-down menu and follow the instructions to get the audio.

We recommend that you download the files directly to your computer, not to your tablet, and extract them there before adding them to your media library. You can then put them onto your tablet, iPod or burn them to CD. On the download page there are instructions and we also provide technical support via the contact form.

For over 350 Free Guitar Lessons with Videos Check Out

www.fundamental-changes.com

Join our Facebook Community of cool musicians

www.facebook.com/groups/fundamentalguitar

Instagram: **FundamentalChanges**

Routine One – Foundation Review

First up, we're going to do a quick review of material from the previous book, to make sure we're all on the same page. Everything we work on in this book will build on these ideas. If this routine is a shock to you, however, don't worry! Just grab a copy of the foundations book and power through it to get up to speed.

I want these routines to be challenging, but nothing you can't have down in an hour. If you find a routine is taking longer than that to master, it's likely you've jumped ahead too quickly.

We'll begin with what many people think of as "classic music school exercises" of the kind historically taught at Berklee and similar establishments. They don't sound particularly musical because they're not! I'm not a huge fan of these myself, but there's no doubt they're very efficient for working on finger dexterity and pick control.

In the first example we're going to play the classic 1234 finger pattern and use it as a way of both warming up our picking hand and getting control of our legato technique.

The technique I like my students to focus on here is, "finger goes down, pick hits string", as it's primarily a synchronisation exercise. Play this with a metronome set to a comfortable speed for you. Before you even make contact with the strings, get your pick moving down and up in time with the metronome as you count in. The aim is to make your picking hand the *heartbeat* that your fretting hand locks into.

In this exercise, alternate pick the notes on the sixth string with a down-up-down-up motion, then use hammer-ons for the notes on the fifth string. Then pick the notes on the fourth string and use hammer-ons for the third string, and so on.

Focus on consistent accurate picking and, for the legato parts, make sure all four notes sound clearly and that you don't run out of steam when hammering on with the fourth finger.

Example 1a:

One of the most frustrating areas of study with my students is rhythm skills and rhythm reading. It's worth noting that while I'm a good sight reader, I don't teach most of my students to read, as it's not a skill they need, and our time is better spent elsewhere. If you're thinking of learning to read music, first ask yourself why, then ask yourself if that time would be better spent on ear training.

That said, I'm a firm believer in learning to read *rhythm*. TAB will always tell you where to put your fingers, but never how long to put them there for, so we need to be able to take more information from the page.

Example 1b is a rhythm reading and strumming exercise that contains 1/4 notes and 1/8th notes. These are simple rhythms that you should be able to read without copying what you hear. Keep the picking hand moving down and up, and hit the strings in the correct places.

Example 1b:

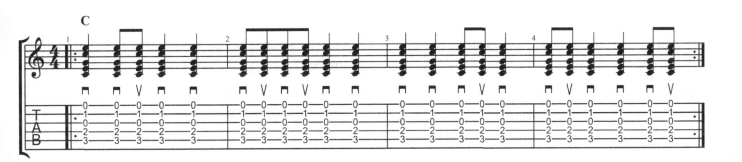

Here's a similar idea that uses more 1/8th notes, this time applied to an A minor chord.

Remember, when strumming that 1/4 notes will always be played with a *down* strum, but 1/8th notes will be played *down-up*.

Example 1c:

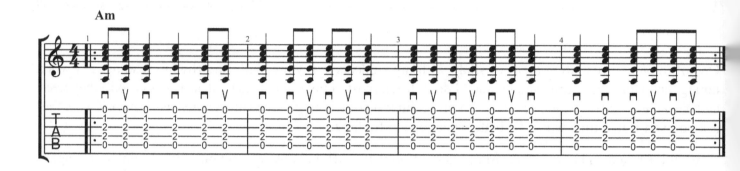

Let's move on to some more complicated rhythm reading. We're still dealing with 1/4 and 1/8th notes here, but now the rhythms are syncopated.

Syncopation is where we place emphasis on an up beat and skip the down beat. For example, in bar one (counting 1 & 2 & 3 & 4 &) you'll play a downstroke on beat 1, hit an upstroke on beat 1&, then skip beat 2. You'll hit an upstroke on beat 2&, then land right on beat 4 with a downstroke. You can see the strumming direction indicated in the TAB.

The struggle most players have with this at first is keeping the picking hand moving down and up, and not contacting the strings when we want to miss out a downstroke.

Spend some time internalising these rhythms. You should be able to count them from the page confidently before you add the complication of your instrument.

Example 1d:

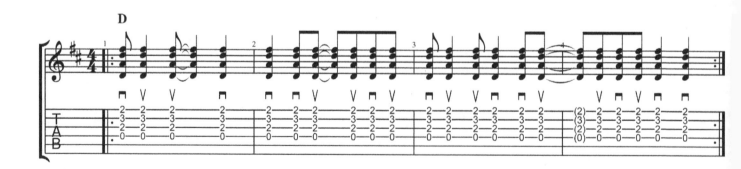

The next recap exercise trains us to confidently play around the Circle of 4ths. We're going to strum through it using E, A and C barre chord shapes.

The Circle of 4ths can be thought of as music's natural order. Beginning with a C chord, we move up a 4th interval to F, then from F we move up another 4th to Bb, and so on. Eventually, we end up back where we started on C, having cycled through all twelve keys.

C – F – Bb – Eb – Ab – Db – F# – B – E – A – D – G – C

Working with the Cycle of 4ths is not only a great way to make sure you practice an idea in every key, it's also what we'd consider a *strong resolution*. In other words, it makes musical sense to our ears.

In order to play this on the guitar, we're using a three-shape cycle. The CAGED C shape moves to the E shape, then to the A shape, then back to the C shape, but higher on the neck. Play through the exercise and get those chord changes nicely under your fingers, so that later, when you play along with me on the audio, it will sound seamless.

Example 1e:

With the chords out of the way, it's time to apply scales to those same positions. Knowing how scales fit around chords is fundamental to the long-term development of your fretboard skills.

This exercise looks easy on the face of it, but it's more difficult than it appears. We'll play just one octave of each scale, so we can change scale from measure to measure. Aim to memorise this. It'll feel like a lot of work to begin with, but the more time you put into it, the more you'll realise that your brain only needs to process the underlying chord shape. The scale will become something automatic, which fits around the chord. In effect, your brain is only having to locate *one thing*, rather than eight different notes.

Example 1f:

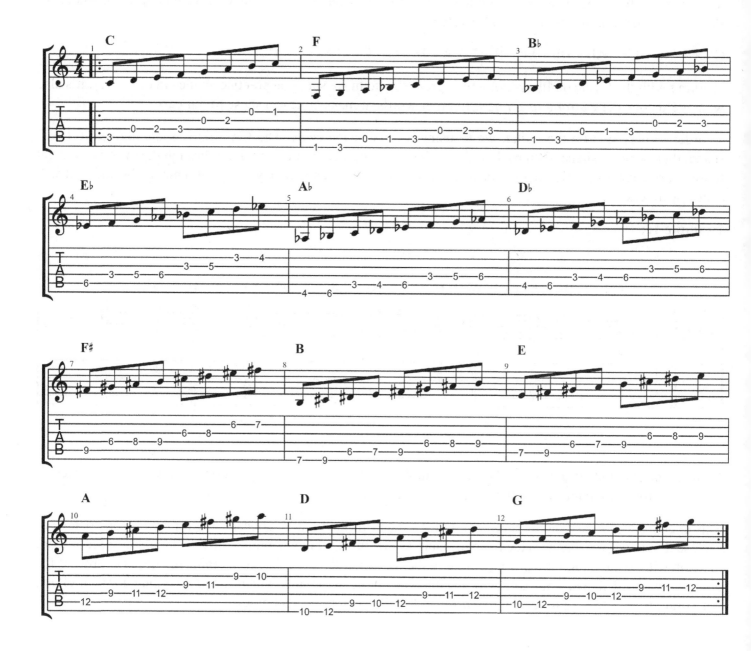

Let's take things a step further and flesh out the basic scale pattern with some musical sequences. These drills are wonderful for both alternate picking practice and breaking up the monotony of playing the same old scales. We'll practice them using the C Major scale.

Here, you'll play the C Major scale using the CAGED A shape in diatonic 3rds, up and down the scale. We'll start on C, skip D, then play an E. Then we'll go back to play the second note in the scale (D), skip E and play F, and so on.

This is an extremely musical sounding exercise that we can work into our soloing quite easily.

Example 1g:

Now we'll play the C Major scale in 3rds again, but this time using the CAGED E shape, starting on the sixth string, 8th fret. This will allow us more fretboard range, so the exercise will be longer.

Example 1h:

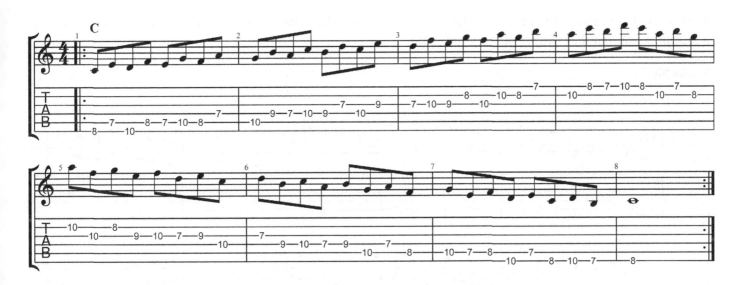

Finally, here's the same 3rds idea, but now using the CAGED C shape in the higher register.

Example 1i:

Of course, there are numerous ways in which we can break up a scale and sequence the notes to make it less monotonous. This exercise uses a four-note pattern. We ascend four notes up the scale, starting on C (C D E F), then go to the second note in the scale and ascend four notes (D E F G), then from the third scale note (E F G A), and so on.

This is another musical and instantly usable sound, but it's also a fabulous alternate picking drill and calls for a lot more stamina that simply playing the scale.

Example 1j:

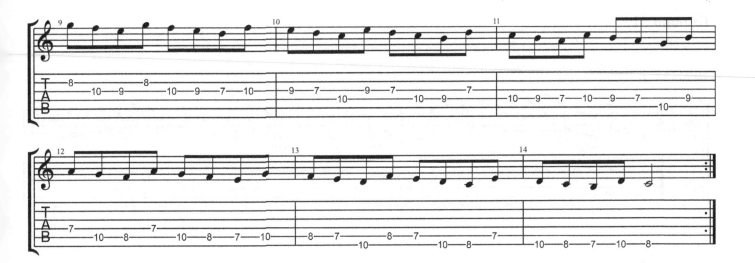

Next we're going to drill cross-picking mechanics for the picking hand. A pattern like this, where the majority of the time there is just one note per string, it's much tricker to play than the patterns we've practiced so far – and infinitely more difficult to play at the same speed, so take your time and learn the movements slowly, committing them to muscle memory.

This exercise reviews triad forms in the key of C Major for the CAGED A, E and C shapes.

Example 1k:

The final recap exercise combines cross-picking and scale sequencing. Here you'll need to cross-pick a C major triad using the E shape, the descend in 3rds in the same position.

Music isn't an exercise, and you'll often be combining different techniques and patterns when playing, so it makes sense to mix them up as much as possible in your practice sessions.

Example 1l:

Whew! That's a lot to get started with, so I'll say it again: if a lot of this stuff is new to you, get hold of the first book in the series and learn it all.

Remember, don't practice until you get it right, practice until you can't get it wrong. If I asked you to play something at random from this chapter's routines, you should be able to do it without hesitation.

E Major, C shape, 3rds… go!

Bb Major, A shape, fours… go!

You get the idea.

Don't shortcut, you'll only end up cheating yourself.

Routine Two – Closed Voiced Triads Primer

My primary focus in my own music education has always been to get increasing control of the instrument and I've found that visualisation is one of the keys to that process.

So far, we've looked at the idea that chord shapes exist around root notes, and scales fit around those chord shapes. Being able to visualise root notes on the fretboard means that you'll quickly be able to find any chord or scale you want to play.

This is a broad view, and it's the first step of many. As you continue to work on your playing, you'll come to realise that this concept is much more nuanced, but each level of mastery will make the previous steps feel much easier.

In this routine we're going to take the next step by working on *closed voice triads*. These are my go-to grips when playing rhythm guitar parts, playing arpeggios, building scales or playing melodic lines.

So, what is a closed voiced triad?

A *triad* describes three notes stacked in 3rds, representing the root, 3rd and 5th of a chord. A C major triad, for example, contains the notes C, E, and G.

However, if we play C major as a barre chord using the CAGED E shape, we end up playing the following six notes: C G C E G C.

Triads only have three notes, so you can see we're doubling up notes here. That doesn't stop this chord from representing a triad, but it has more notes than we need, so we can break it down into smaller, more usable fragments called closed voice triads.

A closed voice triad consists of three notes played in *sequential order* within the span of an octave. For example, if we list the notes of the C major triad over and over…

C E G C E G C E G C E G C E G C

…we can take any three adjacent notes to form a closed voice triad. E.g. C E G or G C E.

(NB: if we took three notes from the list in *non-sequential order*, that's called an open voiced triad).

In Routine One, we practiced three barre chord forms of C major (the A, E and C shapes from the CAGED system). Using those chord forms, we can break each one into four smaller triad voicings.

This means that from just three positions we can learn *twelve* triad fragments incredibly quickly. And now, instead of being limited to playing C major in three ways, we'll have twelve options at our fingertips. Work on this idea and your rhythm playing will take a quantum leap forward.

First, let's quickly recap the three barre chord forms. Play C major using the A shape, E shape, C shape and back to the E shape, then repeat.

Example 2a:

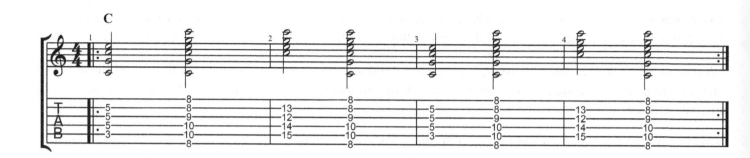

Now let's take this idea and transpose it to the key of G. Remember the visualisation process: look for the root note on the sixth or fifth string, then build the chord shape around it.

This time play the E shape, C shape, A shape, back to the C shape, and repeat.

Example 2b:

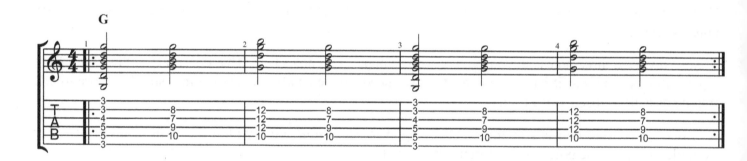

We'll stay in the key of G and work with these three shapes to play smaller, closed voice triads.

Let's begin with the E shape barre chord.

You'll quickly see that the closed voice triads are spelled out by the bigger barre chord form – we're just breaking it apart and playing it on smaller string sets.

The G major triad has the notes G, B, D, and you can see in the example below that the top three strings of the barre form have the notes G, D, B, from high to low.

If we take the G note that was on top and move it to the bottom of that voicing, we get a G major closed voice triad on the second, third and fourth strings (D, B, G high to low).

Now if we take the high D note on the second string and move it down an octave onto the fifth string, we have another closed voice triad on the third, fourth and fifth strings (B, G, D, high to low).

If we repeat this process one more time and move the high B note down an octave, we get a final closed voice triad on the fourth, fifth and sixth strings (G, D, B, high to low).

It may look like these voicings shift up the neck a little, as the lowest note ends up on the 7th fret, while the first fragment is at the 3rd fret. This might make it feel harder to remember, but play this exercise as written for just five minutes each day and it'll be in your muscle memory in no time.

Example 2c:

Next, we're going to repeat this idea with the C shape of the G major barre chord. Once again, you'll quickly see that these smaller closed voiced triads spell out the C shape barre chord pretty clearly, so we can use that form to quickly access any of these smaller triad shapes.

Example 2d:

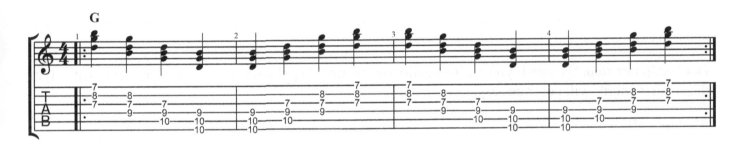

Finally, here are the closed voice triad shapes that come from the A shape barre chord of G major. Like the E shape, this one shifts up the neck slightly.

Example 2e:

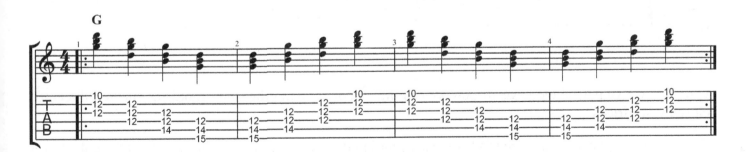

Back when I laid this out on the guitar for the first time, I called the system "undeniable neck geometry" because it's so clear how the triads fall on the fretboard across these three positions.

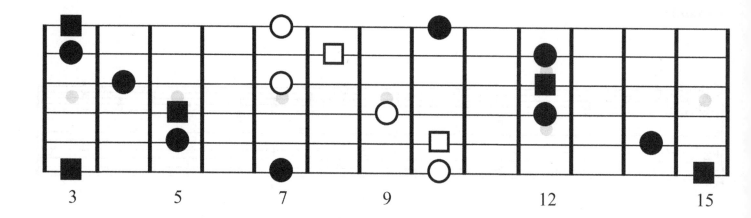

Use this diagram to help strengthen your visualisation of the shapes.

In order to practice this idea, I like to apply these voicings to different chord progressions to keep me on my toes.

In this routine we're going to play through the sequence G major – C major – D major – F major.

To keep them in a similar area of the fretboard, we can use the E shape, A shape, C shape, and the E shape again to play the chords.

Don't skip this step, because if you can't visualise the big chords (which is supposed to be easy) then playing the smaller chords will never be easy!

Example 2f:

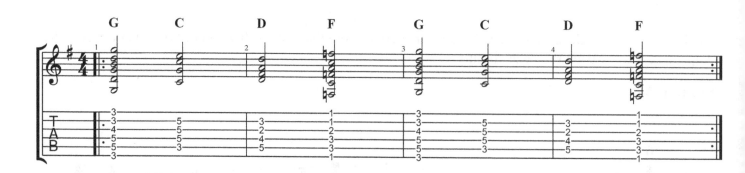

Now that we've played the large shapes, we can think about playing the same chords as smaller, three-note closed voice triads.

We're going to play closed voice triads for each chord in the sequence on all string sets apart from the lowest strings. Triads on the bottom strings can sound a bit muddy, especially in a band setting.

Example 2g:

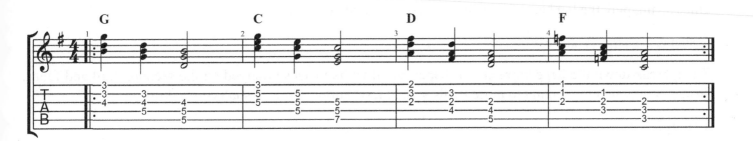

Once you've explored the triad voicings in each position, you can work out how to play the progression on just one string set. This is essentially a voice leading exercise – the idea of moving from chord to chord with the smallest amount of movement.

Here's how to play this progression using just the second, third and fourth strings. This is my favourite string set for rhythm work, as the guitar sounds just great in this register.

Confronted with this idea at face value, if you're struggling to visualise where it comes from, go back and make sure you can "see" the larger barre chord shapes, before picking out the smaller parts.

Example 2h:

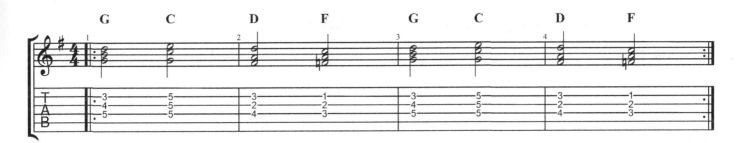

Let's do the same thing again, this time using the top three strings. The guitar sounds thinner here, but these voicings are ideal to cut through a band mix. Alternatively, add some delay effect and a volume pedal, and you've got something really musical that sounds a bit like a keyboard part.

Example 2i:

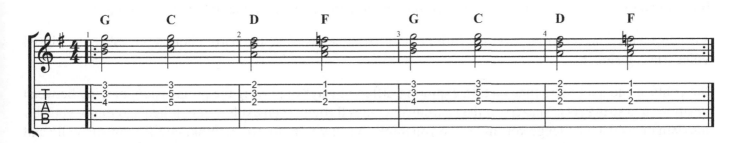

Now we're going to move to another position of the neck and do it all again. The last loop started in the E shape, so now we're going to do it starting in the C shape.

Once again, play the big barre forms first (this part should be easy).

C shape, E shape, A shape, C shape

Then, break down the large barre chord shapes and dive into triads arranged on the second, third and fourth strings. Immediately jumping to those triads should test/reinforce your visualisation skills.

Example 2j:

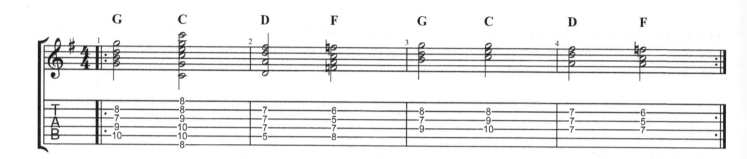

Let's do it again, now starting in the A shape. We'll play,

A shape, C shape, E shape, A shape.

First play the big barre chords, then the smaller, closed voiced triads.

Example 2k:

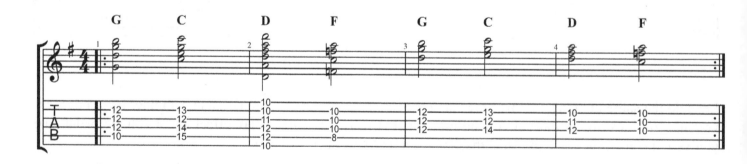

You can see how this approach logically unfolds. In the final exercise we move between positions on the neck but stay on the second-third-fourth string set. As you play through this, remember how we got here:

Visualise barre chord root note on the fifth or sixth string > visualise the barre chord > visualise the closed voice triads inside it

We could spend a lot more time on this, exploring different ways of playing the progression, moving between positions and string sets. Mastery of the instrument comes through such exploration. It helps to throw yourself into situations that challenge you and make you think. When you're forced to think, you'll grow mentally and add to your understanding – and that's where the real growth is.

Example 21:

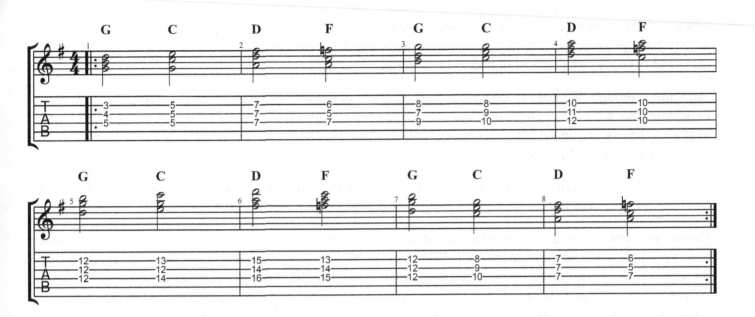

I can't stress strongly enough the importance of this routine. Closed voice triads lie at the core of everything I teach on the guitar. When students come to me for lessons, this is what we do in our first few sessions, because if you don't know this stuff, you're going to hit a wall at some point.

Repeat this routine as many times as you need until you don't have to think about it anymore. It needs to become automatic. The work is worth it.

Routine Three – Dominating Dominant 7s

I like to think of triad harmony as the basic ingredients of a cake we're making. There's nothing wrong with a tasty jam sponge cake – in fact, sometimes that's exactly what we want. Likewise, there are hundreds of thousands of songs that consist of nothing but triads.

Sometimes though, we want to add other ingredients to our cake to make something different. How about a chocolate cake with icing? Or a carrot cake? Both have things in common with the basic cake, but there's more going on. The "icing on the cake" is how I like to think of 7th chords. They're like basic triads but with added ingredients to create different flavours.

In this routine we're going to look at the dominant 7 chord sound and work through how to build it from our triad knowledge, how to turn it into an arpeggio, and finally into a larger scale/mode.

Dominant 7 chords are a fundamental part of many types of music. You'll see them often as the V chord in chord progressions and they are the basis of more than 80% of blues and gospel music. Since rock music has its roots in the blues, you can expect dominant sounds to form the basis of most of the classic rock that was influenced by the blues. To me, this sound is even more important than the major scale, as it forms the basis of what I'm going to play over just about any *major* type chord as well as dominant chords.

We'll get to this in due course, but first, a triad picking warmup.

First up, we're going to play a descending fours pattern using an E shaped C major triad. After playing two groups of four descending, we'll ascend from the bottom back up to the top using the C Major scale. This will give you a nice picking workout, but will also allow you to visualise how these two things are interlinked.

Example 3a:

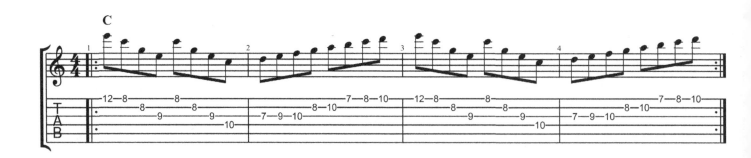

Here's a similar idea, but this time we connect the ascending C Major scale to a descending F major triad in the C shape.

Mixing chords and scales together like this is a great way to explore the fretboard while keeping your technique sharp.

Example 3b:

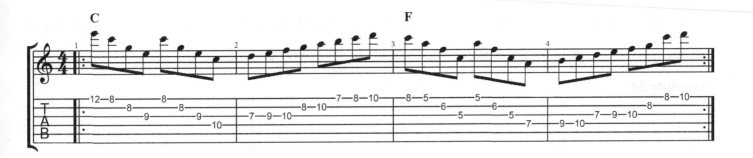

With the warmup done, it's time for the dominant 7 sound. So, what *is* a dominant 7 chord?

Simply put, it's a major triad with a b7 note added to it. But let's get theoretical for a second, then make it real simple.

What's the b7 note, Levi?

I could say, it's the 7th degree of the major scale lowered a half step. The chord C7 is therefore made up of a C major triad (C E G) plus a Bb note. (The 7th note in the C Major scale is B, so Bb is a half step below that).

This is an accurate technical explanation, but practically speaking there's a *much* easier way memorise and, more importantly, locate the b7:

Take your root note and move down a half step and you're at the 7th. Move it down another half step and you're at the b7 note.

In Example 3c we're going to play C major as a barre chord in the three positions we've practiced. Then we'll take one of the higher C notes and move it down to Bb to give us a C7 chord.

This exercise is useful to help you learn C7 voicings, understand where they come from, and how to construct them.

Example 3c:

Now let's look at dominant 7 chords in a progression.

We'll play the common soul sequence, C major – D7 – F major – C major

The first time through, we'll play the D7 chord using our C shape, then with the A shape the second time through.

(In your own time, try playing this idea using the E shape for the D7 chord too!)

Example 3d:

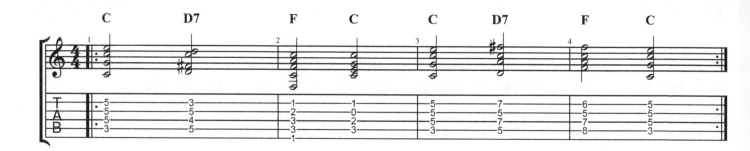

Here's another soul chord progression:

A major – C#7 – D major – D minor

In this example we're playing the C#7 chord using the A shape. Again, this could (and should) be played in lots of different positions. Your goal is to be fluent enough on the fretboard that you're able to play a chord progression anywhere on the neck.

As a separate exercise, play examples 3d and 3e swapping the dominant 7 chords for plain major triads. The effect is remarkable as they instantly sound pretty plain. Dominant 7 chords are an important tool for creating specific flavours in our rhythm work.

Example 3e:

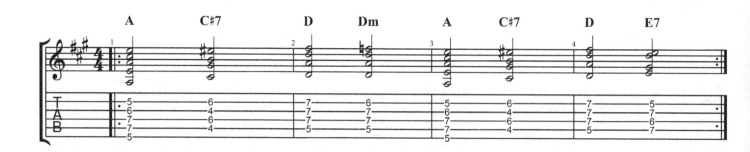

Here's a final chord progression that's a little longer. This one uses both an F7 chord (C shape) and a C7 chord (E shape).

F – Dm – F – Dm F7 – Bb – C7 – F

This exercise is a great example of how dominant 7 chords often work in songs. Notice that the F7 chord resolves to a Bb chord, and the C7 chord resolves to F. What is the significance of this?

Remember the Circle of 4ths?

C – F – Bb – Eb – Ab – Db – F# - B – E – A – D – G – C

I mentioned earlier that we consider the interval of a 4th to be a strong sounding resolution. Well, the dominant 7 chord just helps to emphasise that strong motion, adding some tension before the resolution.

Example 3f:

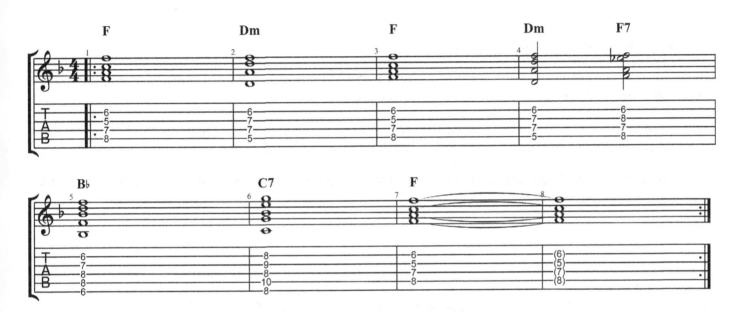

I've spoken about the prevalence of the dominant 7 chord in blues music. In this genre, it's very common to solo over dominant 7 chords with minor pentatonic scales. Let's look at these two things side by side.

C7 = C E G Bb

C Minor Pentatonic = C Eb F G Bb

Immediately, you may notice the clear clash between the E note in the chord and the Eb note in the scale. To account for this, blues players often tend to bend the Eb note slightly sharp to bring it more in line with the chord (but not always, and many blues players freely mix licks with major 3rds and minor 3rds).

In Example 3g, we'll play a C7 chord followed by the C Minor Pentatonic scale, first in the lower octave then in the higher octave. Each time, the scale pattern will come to rest on the b3 (Eb), so you can hear how that tension sounds.

Example 3g:

Now it's time to look at dominant 7 arpeggios.

Remember, arpeggios are just the notes of a chord played in a linear fashion. I think of arpeggio shapes as skeletons, which we can flesh out to make scales and create melodies.

In this example we're going to play the basic arpeggio triad ascending (C E G), then drop down to play the b7 (Bb). This will give us our basic arpeggio fingerings and sounds for C7 in our A, E, and C shapes.

You'll notice that the b7 note appears in the same place as it did in the earlier chord voicings, because all these things are connected.

Example 3h:

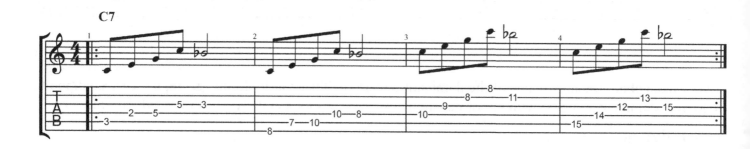

Now that you've played these smaller fragments and got the sound of the dominant 7 arpeggio in your ears, play through the A, E and C shapes of C7 in full.

Once again, we first play the chord then the arpeggio ascending and descending, to strengthen the relationship between the two. This is a great alternate picking workout. Try to allow the picking to be automatic and keep your focus on the placement of the b7 in each of these positions – that note is really important.

Example 3i:

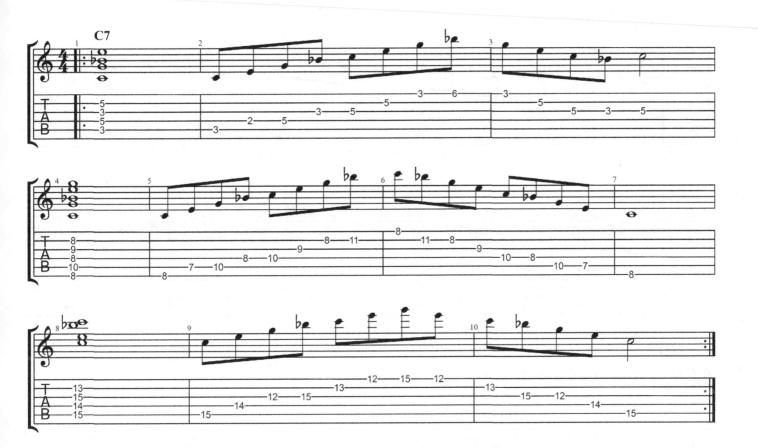

Next we're going to apply these dominant 7 arpeggios to a 12-bar blues progression in the key of C.

This exercise will help to strengthen your visualisation of the arpeggio over the chord, and give you the extra challenge of having to look ahead to the next chord. It would be easy to take one shape and move it up/ down the neck to fit the current chord (it's a valid approach and one that I might use sometimes) but why not challenge ourselves to stay in one area of the neck and use three arpeggio shapes?

Example 3j:

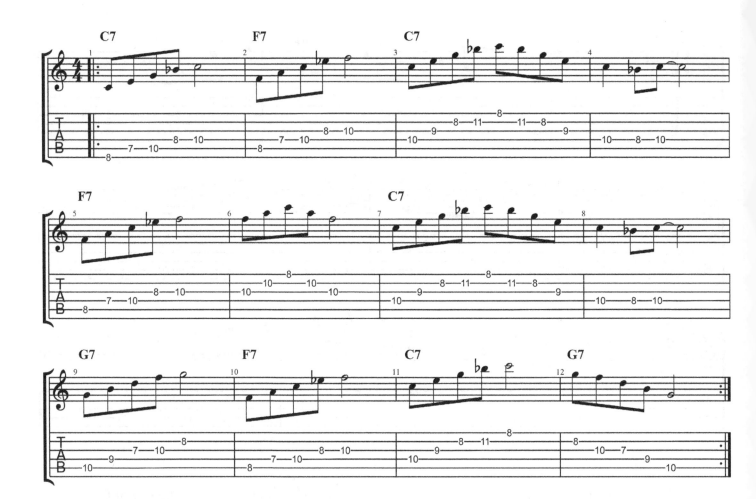

Next, let's look at scales. What scale should we play over a dominant 7 chord?

Although a dominant 7 chord is a major triad plus a b7, we can't play the major scale over it because it has a major 7 which will clash with the b7.

So, what if we simply lower the major scale's 7 to a b7 and leave the rest of the notes the same?

I call this the "dominant scale" because it perfectly fits a dominant 7 chord. I got that from the great Ted Greene. Why call a scale something complicated when we can name it after how we'll use it? A music theorist would call it the mixolydian mode, but what does that *mean*? We have to translate that for it to mean something, whereas *the dominant scale* spells out a dominant 7 chord.

In Example 3k, play the C Dominant scale in the A shape. It's just like the C Major scale you already know, but with the 7 (B) lowered to a b7 (Bb).

Example 3k:

You can probably guess where this is going, because we need to know this in all our positions! Here's the E shape.

Example 3l:

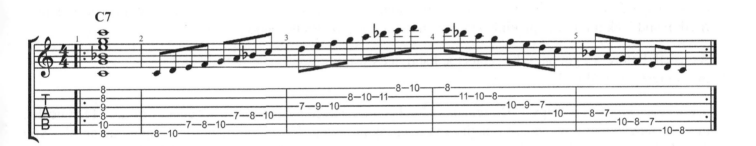

And finally, the C shape.

Example 3m:

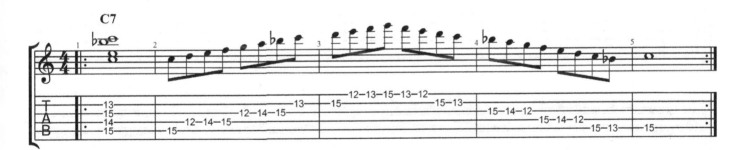

Take your time to program in these fingerings and sounds, because they're going to be the basis of a lot of things you play in your musical future.

Good work, and I'll see you in a week!

Routine Four – Sixteenth Note Primer

I've given you a lot of pitch work and theory over the last couple of weeks, so this week we're going to give that side of the brain a rest while we deal with some rhythmic concepts and get our picking hand ready for some funk!

Until now, we've only played exercises using 1/4 notes or 1/8th notes. An 1/8th note is half the length of a 1/4 note, so you could say it splits each beat into two notes. If we split those 1/8th notes in half again, we have four notes per beat and we call these 1/16th notes.

1/16th notes are just as important a rhythm as 1/4 and 1/8th notes and come up just as often, regardless of the style of music you play, so we need to have them down.

It's a mistake to think of 1/16th notes as "faster" than 1/8th notes because it's all relative. 1/8th notes played at 300 beats per minute are faster than 1/16th notes at 100bpm. They are just different rhythmic subdivisions; different ways of dividing the beat to create interesting rhythms.

That said, as the tempo increases, you'll be playing twice as many notes, and to play continuous 1/16th notes calls for good control in the picking hand and some stamina. We also need to learn how to read this new rhythm and lock it into our picking hand, so that it all becomes automatic.

As usual, before we get onto the subject at hand, let's warm up our picking hand and refresh our memory on the content covered in the last routine.

We'll begin with the E shape, C Dominant scale, this time played by applying a sequence of fours. Technically, this is a new exercise we've not practiced yet, but by now you should find that you're applying an idea you already know to a scale you already know. Hopefully you won't find it much of a problem!

Example 4a:

Now, using the same position, play through the scale ascending and descending in diatonic 3rds. This shouldn't be too tricky. If you're struggling with this being automatic, it can only mean one of two things: 1) you don't know the scale pattern well enough, or, 2) you don't know how the sequence works well enough. You can easily work on both of those!

Example 4b:

With the warmup done, let's look at some 1/16th note rhythms with some basic strumming ideas.

So far, we've been used to strumming and picking 1/8th notes with alternate down-up picking. 1/16th notes kicks that up a gear.

While we count a bar of 1/8th notes as,

"1 & 2 & 3 & 4 &"

We count a bar of 1/16th notes as,

"1 e & a, 2 e & a, 3 e & a, 4 e & a"

Instead of one beat equalling "1 &" (a down-up strum or pick)

With 1/16th notes one beat equals "1 e & a" (down-up-down-up)

Let's look at that again. Below I've written out a 1/16th note rhythm, highlighting the 1/16th notes in brackets:

"1 (e) & (a), 2 (e) & (a)"

Picking wise we'll play that,

Down (up) down (up), down (up) down (up)

What I'm getting at here is that if you play music that contains both 1/8th notes and 1/16th notes, all the 1/8th notes should be played as downstrokes, so that you don't have to change gears when playing 1/16th notes – your picking/strumming mechanic will already be in place.

Let's begin by practicing with a small G7 chord voicing.

You can see the 1/16th notes mapped out in bar one below. With your picking hand, you'll strum every 1/16th note, but your fretting hand will only sound some of them.

Apply some fretting hand pressure to sound the first 1/16th note and the other 1/16th notes as indicated. Lift the fretting hand slightly to mute the strings for all 1/16th notes marked with an X. Don't remove your fretting hand from the strings at any point, just apply and release the pressure.

Now look at the picking hand. The goal here is to have a nice, relaxed picking hand and wrist, playing a constant down-up-down-up pattern.

After doing this for a bar, keep the exact same motion in both hands, but this time don't strike the muted strings. You can see in the notation I've included three rests with pick stoke indications, because the picking hand should keep moving.

When you want to play something funky (as in bar one), you'll strum the strings constantly and control the muting. When you want to pick out chord stabs (as in bar two), you'll keep the strumming motion going but won't make contact with the strings, apart from playing the stabs.

Example 4c:

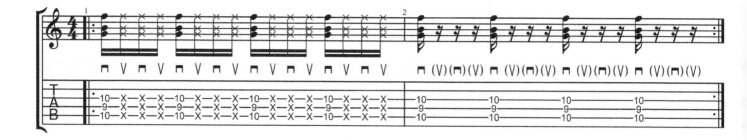

Let's try that exercise again, but with a trickier rhythm. This time, instead of playing the first of each group of 1/16th notes, we'll pick out the second. In other words, one beat of music will be played,

Mute-chord-mute-mute

Strumming-wise, the first mute will be a downstroke and you'll hit the chord on the upstroke.

When we remove those muted strums, the rhythm becomes a little trickier. From a technical perspective it should be no different – the picking hand is still constantly strumming down and up – but many students struggle with not contacting the strings on the downstrokes. This may feel awkward at first, but it's increasing your control over the instrument, and that's the goal.

Example 4d:

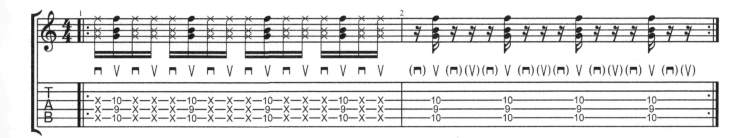

Now we're going to do the same thing again but this time picking out the third 1/16th note in each group. As you might expect, this accent is going to fall on a downstroke.

Example 4e:

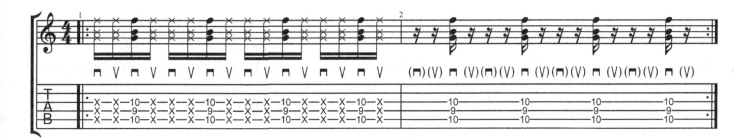

Finally, let's do the same thing, but now hitting the final 1/16th note of each group with an upstroke.

Example 4f:

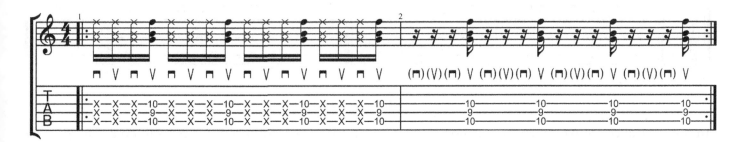

The last few exercises were designed to get the continuous 1/16th note strumming motion in place. Now it's time to move on to some single note picking exercises, which we'll play while working on our rhythm reading.

The idea is simple: we'll take a rhythm, apply it to a single note, and read it over and over.

When playing these exercises, don't take your eyes off the page. You're learning to understand the rhythm and training your brain to be able to *see* a rhythm and know exactly what it will sound like. You're also training your picking hand to know how to execute it.

Once we've worked on the single note idea, we'll apply 1/16th note rhythms to a melody. You will find that once you've programmed in the rhythm, you can devote almost all of your brain's processing power to playing the correct notes.

First up, we'll start easy – just straight 1/16th notes.

Example 4g:

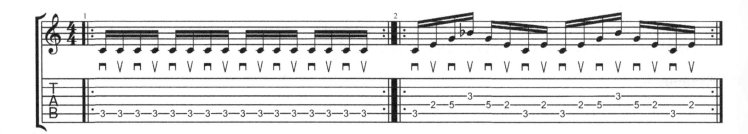

Now we'll do the same with a rhythm of an 1/8th note followed two 1/16th notes. Notice that the picking pattern here is *down-down-up*. Don't stop that pick moving – there's a downstroke, then the pick comes up while you're holding the 1/8th note, then you pick *down-up* for the two 1/16th notes.

This is often referred to as the gallop rhythm and you'll hear why.

Example 4h:

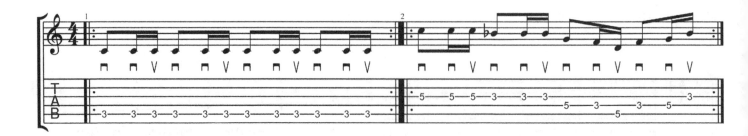

In the next exercise we reverse the gallop to play two 1/16th notes followed by an 1/8th note. The picking pattern will be *down-up-down*.

Again, don't cheat yourself, put in as much time as you need before moving ahead. If you're not reading the rhythms, you're not getting any better!

Example 4i:

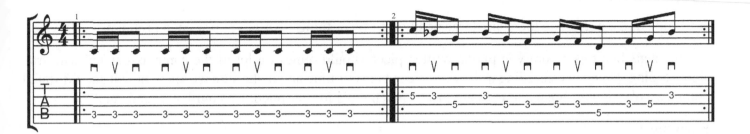

Next, we have a syncopated rhythm that alternates 1/16th, 1/8th, 1/16th.

This is a neglected rhythm as it's upstroke heavy, but if you know that's a weakness for you, then it's what you should focus on, not ignore!

Example 4j:

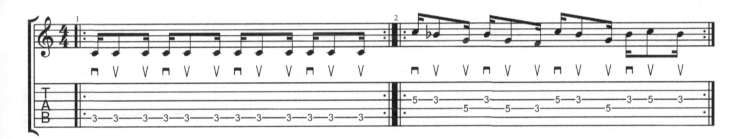

We've done lots of work to keep our picking hand motion consistent, but now we're going to throw that out the window to work on hearing different rhythmic subdivisions.

In this exercise, we're going to alternate pick between 1/8th notes, triplets, 1/16th notes, and back to triplets. This is really a counting exercise. If you can accurately count this, you should be able to play it.

1 &, 2 &, 3 & a, 4 & a, 1 e & a, 2 e & a, 3 & a, 4 & a

Whew!

Example 4k:

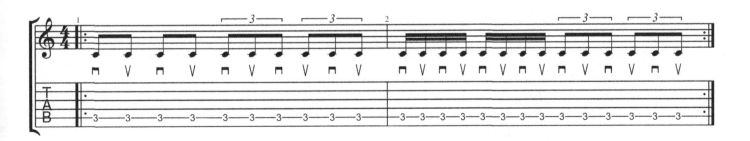

After reading and playing various 1/16th note rhythms, this final example is a reading exercise that brings together most of the rhythms you've worked on. Before you attempt to play it, just take a look through it. Do any of the rhythms scare you? Could you count it?

Now look at the notes. Are there any large position shifts or things that might present a problem?

Taking steps like this before you play a written piece should remove a lot of the panic associated with true sight reading. No one is recording us here – we can take our time and make sure we know how it should sound before we play it. Our brain and eyes are just as much tools for our playing as our hands and ears!

Example 4l:

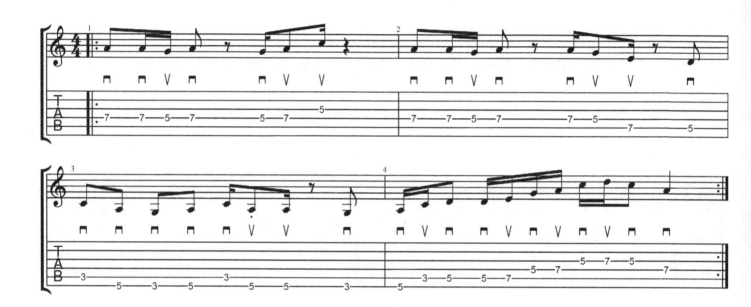

I place a lot of value on rhythmic comprehension. As a transcriber, this is the most important skill for me. Anyone can work out the notes they hear, but writing rhythm is always going to be tricker. It makes sense that if I can read a rhythm and know what it's going to sounds like, I should be able to *hear* a rhythm and know what it should *look* like!

Get to work and I'll see you in a week.

Routine Five – Major and Minor Sevenths

In the previous routine, I said that the dominant 7 chord sound forms the basis of most of the music you'll play as a blues, rock, or country musician. But it's not the only sound available and there are plenty of other musical genres to explore.

Pop, jazz, Latin, soul, and many other types of music are rich in both major and minor 7 chords, so they're something we should have under our belt. We need to know them when we hear them, and know how to play them when the musical situation demands it.

In this routine we're going to get to grips with "shell voicings". Learning these means you'll be set up to play any major 7, minor 7, or dominant 7 chord without hesitation – all you need to do is locate the root note.

It stands to reason that if you're able to play a chord, you should be able to play it as an arpeggio too, without any real problem, so we'll do that too!

But first… a warmup based on last week's routine.

In this example we'll play a small G7 chord voicing with a funk strumming technique. The challenge in this exercise is that we're not playing the chord accent in the same place each time.

In the first group of 1/16th notes we sound the first and the fourth note (**1** e & **a**).

In the second group, it's just the third note of beat two (1 e **&** a).

In the third group, it's the second note of beat three (1 **e** & a).

In the fourth group, it's just the first note of beat four (**1** e & a)

This is an interesting rhythm and it's really the fretting hand that's executing it via muting, as the picking hand is hitting the strings on every 1/16th note. If you want to make this one sound a little more musical, you could play a little softer with the picking hand on all of the muted notes.

Example 5a:

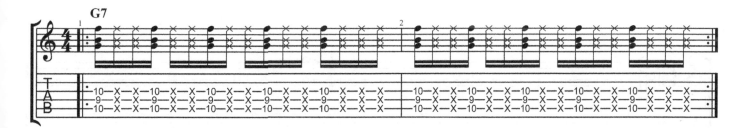

Now let's prepare for the material ahead by playing G7 and C7 chords using the E, C, and A shapes. You need to be able to play these automatically before we can build on them.

Example 5b:

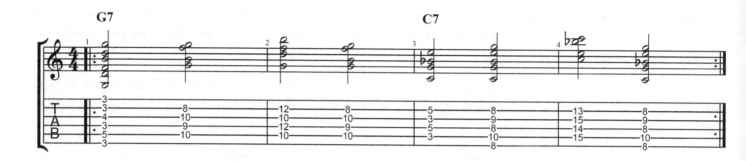

Notice that these chord voicings contain lots of notes, some of them doubled.

Remember that a dominant 7 chord contains four intervals: root, 3rd, 5th and b7.

Let's pause for a moment and think about the function each note serves.

The root note grounds the chord – it's what we hear everything else in relation to.

The 3rd tells us if the chord is major or minor.

The 5th doesn't serve any harmonic function, it just makes the chord sound thicker.

The 7th (in conjunction with the 3rd) tells us what type of 7th chord we're playing.

Because of this, we can play just the root, 3rd and 7th of a chord and still identify it as a major 7, minor 7 or dominant 7. In fact, if we happen to be working with a bass player who is playing the root notes, we can get away with playing only the 3rd and 7th to make the sound of the chord!

A root, 3rd, 7th voicing is known as a *shell voicing*.

Here's how they sound applied to G7 in the E and C shapes.

Example 5c:

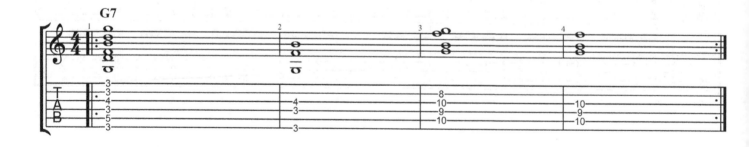

Let's stick with the E shape and play through three different chord types in the same position using shell voicings. We'll move through major 7, dominant 7 and minor 7.

A major 7 chord is a major triad with an added major 7: root, 3rd, 5th, 7th.

A dominant 7 chord is a major triad with an added flattened or minor 7: root, 3rd, 5th, b7.

A minor 7 chord is a minor triad with an added flattened or minor 7: root, b3, 5th, b7.

As we play through the chords, we'll use this knowledge to adapt the shell voicing for each chord. We're leaving out the 5th and adjusting the 3rd and 7th intervals as needed.

We start with a Gmaj7 voiced root, 7th, 3rd.

Then we lower the 7th a half step to a b7 to play G7 voiced root, b7, 3rd.

Next, we move the 3rd down a half step to a b3 to play Gm7 voiced root, b3, b7.

Then we repeat the process to play Cmaj7, C7 and Cm7 chords.

Example 5d:

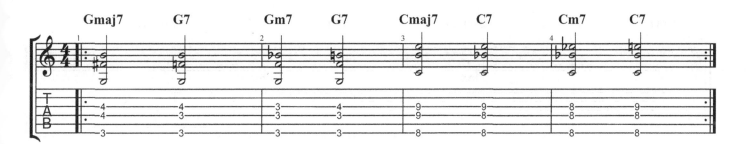

Now let's play the same idea, but with chords that have root notes on the fifth string. We'll swap around the order of the G and C chords so that the voicings ascend the neck. This gives us three more voicings for each chord that we should know.

Example 5e:

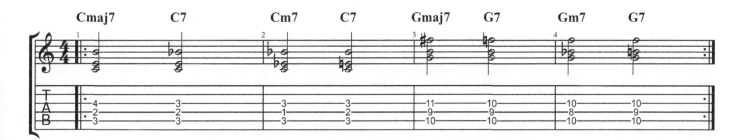

One of the best ways to work on these voicings is by playing the classic ii V I chord progression. In the key of C Major, that's Dm7 (ii) – G7 (V) – Cmaj7 (I). This is a great chord sequence as it includes all three chord types.

The chords alternate between root notes on the fifth and sixth strings. If we start with a fifth string root, the V chord will have its root on the sixth string, and the I chord will be back on the fifth string.

If we start with a sixth string root, the V chord will have its root on the fifth string, and the I chord will be back on the sixth string.

In this example we'll play ii V Is in three different keys. If you want to challenge yourself a bit more, play the progression round the Circle of 4ths in all twelve keys!

Example 5f:

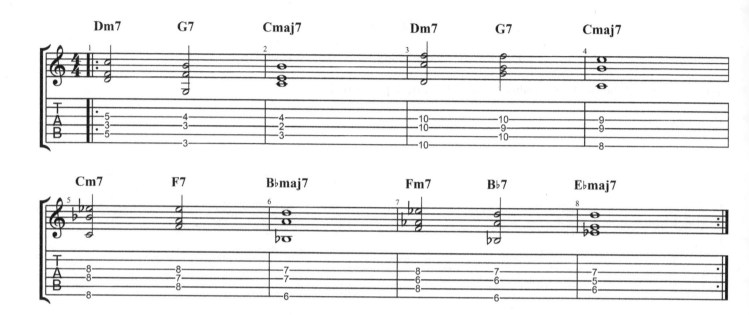

With that simple exercise out of the way, let's apply this idea to some longer chord progressions.

The first one is a sunny, summery progression that features lots of ii V I movements. The more you play this style, the more you'll notice the pattern of minor 7 chords moving up a 4th to a dominant 7 chord, and the dominant 7 moving up a 4th to resolve to a major 7 chord.

Example 5g:

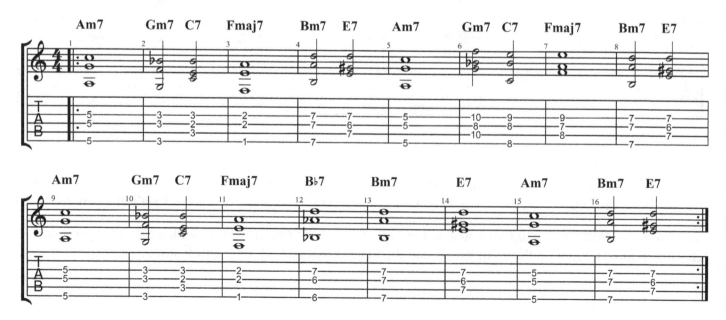

Here's a darker, misty ballad progression, but again you'll see the same movements. You'll be able to do a lot with these chord voicings when you know them inside out.

It's also fascinating to see that the nature of the guitar makes this pretty simple. We don't worry about what the notes are in an Abm7 chord, because we know the physical intervals on our instrument. If you can see the root note, you'll be able to play it.

Example 5h:

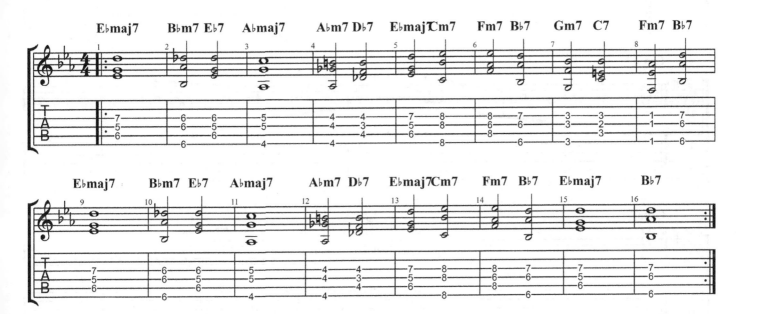

Now we've explored shell voicings, let's move on to play arpeggios in three positions. Remember, arpeggios are just the notes of the chord played in a linear fashion.

Your goal here is to focus on identifying the intervals in relation to the root note as you play them, which will bring you a greater level of control over your instrument.

Let's start with major 7 arpeggios.

Example 5i:

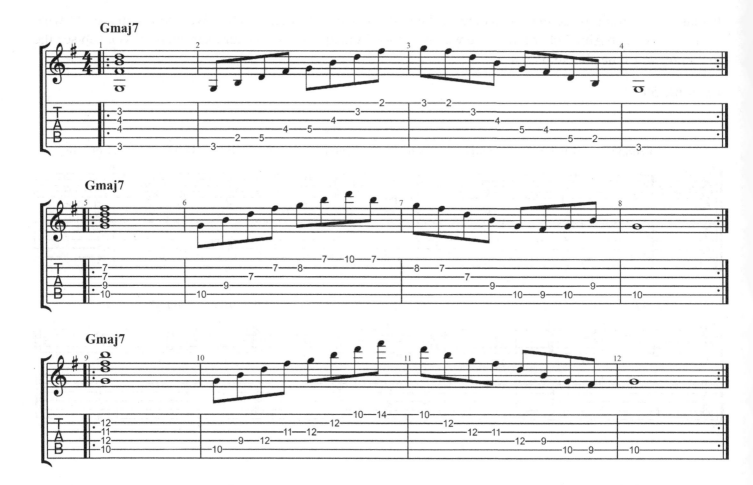

Now do the same with minor 7 arpeggios.

Example 5j:

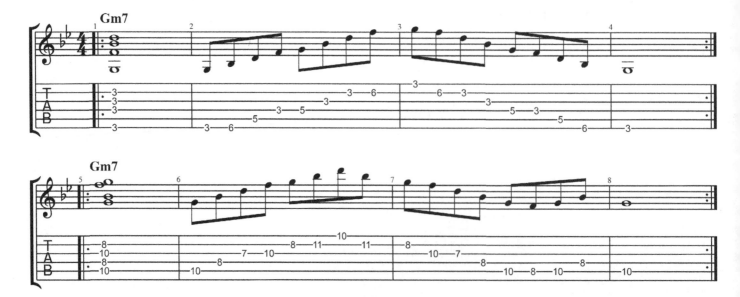

Now you have the fingering down for major and minor arpeggios (you've already drilled dominant 7 arpeggios, so you should know those), let's apply them to some ii V I progressions, first of all in Bb Major.

In bars 1-4 you'll play each arpeggio from the root note, so it's easier to visualise where you're going. Then, in bars 5-8, you'll apply a little more rhythm and contour to the arpeggios to play a simple melody.

Example 5k:

Finally, let's play a similar idea switching to the key of D Major.

As before, you'll begin by playing arpeggios from their root notes, then add rhythm and contour to create something more melodic.

Example 5l:

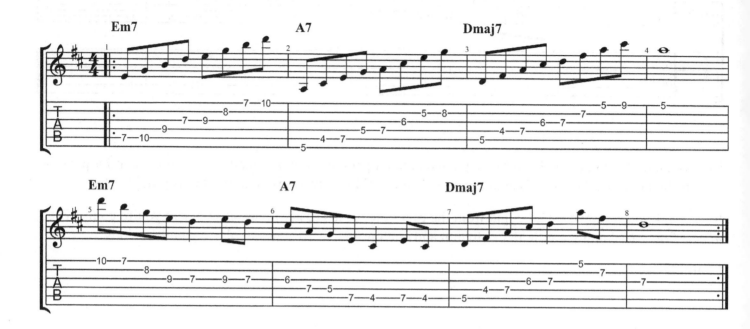

If you want to take this idea further and really nail it, grab yourself a copy of the *Real Book*, and play through different songs spelling out the arpeggios for each chord.

That's it for this week. Get to work and I'll see you in a week's time.

Routine Six – 4ths and 5ths

I've always maintained that playing scales up and down is one of the least efficient uses of our time on the guitar in the practice room. If we spend our lives practicing scales, then we'll just play scales.

In previous routines I introduced the idea of playing sequences as a way of breaking up scale practice. Sequences help us to explore scale positions in more depth, and also present us with some technical hurdles, which will help improve our picking and fretting skills.

The "fours" and diatonic 3rds sequences we've looked at are wonderful, musical ways of breaking up a scale pattern, but today we're going to explore other options and look at diatonic 4ths and 5ths.

Remember that the only way to execute these ideas with minimal effort is to have a rock solid visualisation of the scale patterns. These new intervals will present some technical playing challenges, but they'll also introduce you to some new sounds that you'd almost certainly never play if you just ran up and down scales all day.

We'll start our routine this week by warming up, playing the A Dominant scale in diatonic 3rds. Remember to keep that picking hand nice and relaxed.

Even though this is a single note exercise, do your best to visualise the whole scale pattern, no matter where you are in the sequence.

Example 6a:

Diatonic 4ths

Now let's look at diatonic 4ths.

The A Dominant scale has the notes,

A B C# D E F# G A

The idea is to take the first note (A), move four notes up the scale to play D, then go back and play the second note in the scale (B). From the B note, we move four notes up the scale again to play E, and so on.

When we apply the 4ths pattern to the guitar, we immediately notice that we often have to play notes at the same fret on adjacent strings. This presents a major technical issue with the fretting hand, as we don't want these notes to ring into each other – each note needs to be fretted cleanly.

In order to do this, you need to execute a *finger roll* with the fretting hand. Fret the first note on the sixth string as normal, then roll the finger sideways onto the adjacent fifth string. As you do this, the pressure on the sixth string will be released and the note will stop sounding.

The roll technique is something I've worked on extensively, so I have no problem applying it with all four fingers of the fretting hand. I practiced this a lot in my teens!

Here is the A Dominant scale played in ascending 4ths, while remaining in position.

Example 6b:

When descending the pattern, the roll technique has to work in reverse. You can't fret the note on the first string as you would normally, because when you want to roll onto the second string, there's no more finger to do it! Instead, you need to fret this first note as though you'd already rolled onto it from the second string. This means using more of the pad of the finger, rather than the tip. Now, when you roll over onto the B string, you'll be fretting that note in the traditional fashion.

Example 6c:

One of my favourite ways to make these ideas sound more musical is to mix the intervals and the direction in which they are played.

In this pattern, we start with the A root note, then play D (4th), then E (the next sequential scale note), then B (a 4th interval but descending from the E), then C# (next sequential scale note), then F# (4th) and so on.

Example 6d:

You can also mix up when you ascend and descend these diatonic intervals. In the following exercise, we're working with the exact same scale position, but instead of alternating strictly between descending and ascending intervals we're playing this pattern:

Down, up, down, down, up, down, down, up, down, down, up, down, up, down.

That might sound complicated but play through the pattern and you'll get it. The point of this idea is that it removes the element of predictability that sequences often suffer from, but keeps the "this makes sense to my ears" feeling the listener experiences when you play something they can latch on to.

Example 6e:

We've devoted a little time to the E shape of this scale, but you need to be able to play these sequences anywhere, so now let's work with diatonic 4ths in the C shape.

As always, if you're struggling to keep up, go back and put more time into making sure you know the scale pattern as well as you need to.

Example 6f:

Here's the same idea, but now applied in the A shape. There's nothing new here, you're just seeing it in a different place!

Example 6g:

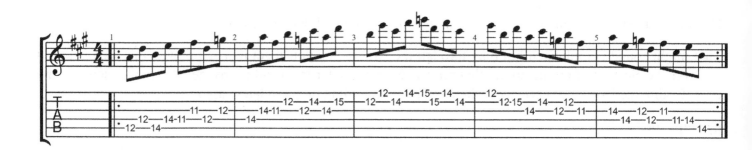

Diatonic 5ths

Diatonic 4ths have always felt incredibly usable to me. They are a big part of the vocabulary of musicians I listen to, from guitar players like Scott Henderson and Frank Gambale, to horn players like Michael Brecker and Joshua Redman.

I've always found 5ths a bit trickier to work into my playing, because they're not quite as common in the soloing of my favourite players. However, Joe Diorio was a big fan of 5ths, and you certainly hear them a fair amount in more modern jazz players like Julian Lage and Jonathan Kreisberg.

You can see this as a downside or a positive. By working with them, it means you'll stand out a little more from other players.

Here are diatonic 5ths applied to the E shape in ascending form.

Example 6h:

And now the same in descending form. Take note of the tricky string crosses that require you to skip a string while inside picking. Manoeuvres like this can present problems, so drilling them in our practice routines is essential.

Example 6i:

As we did with 4ths, we can mix up the direction of the intervals to remove the sense of predictability from the pattern and keep the listener guessing. In this example we're alternating between ascending and descending as we move down the scale position.

Example 6j:

Here are diatonic 5ths in the C shape. There's nothing new here, we're just applying the concept to the scale pattern in a different zone of the neck.

Example 6k:

Finally, here's the scale ascending and descending in 5ths up in the A shape.

Example 6l:

That's it for this routine. We've covered a lot of ground and we've only just scratched the surface of what's possible.

You've learned a series of useful scale patterns and sequences, but only applied them to one key. You could easily mix other scales into your practice sessions or apply these ideas to the Circle of 4ths. That's the beauty of practice routines, they can be customised to fit your needs and focus on your problem areas.

Get to work, and I'll see you in a week!

Routine Seven – Double-Stops & Soul

Last week was really hard work! Maybe it felt like we were so caught up in the exercises that we forgot what this is all about – making music. In this routine we're going to fix that by turning all the triad concepts we've learned into very musical ideas.

There's a definite emphasis on soul music here, as that's my main gig these days. But while this stuff is wonderful when you're trying to sound like Steve Cropper or Cornell Dupree, it's worth remembering that these ideas were also fundamental to the playing of great blues and rock players like Stevie Ray Vaughn and Jimi Hendrix. There's also a lot of crossover into the country world here, so there's value for just about any player.

As well as triad work, we're going to look at moving between positions and connecting them with double-stops.

Before we get into it, let's refresh our memory of the twelve small closed voice triads we worked with in three positions. We'll alternate pick through them all with a triplet feel.

We're never going to have to play something like this in a song, but it's challenging enough to constitute a nice technical and mental warmup.

Example 7a:

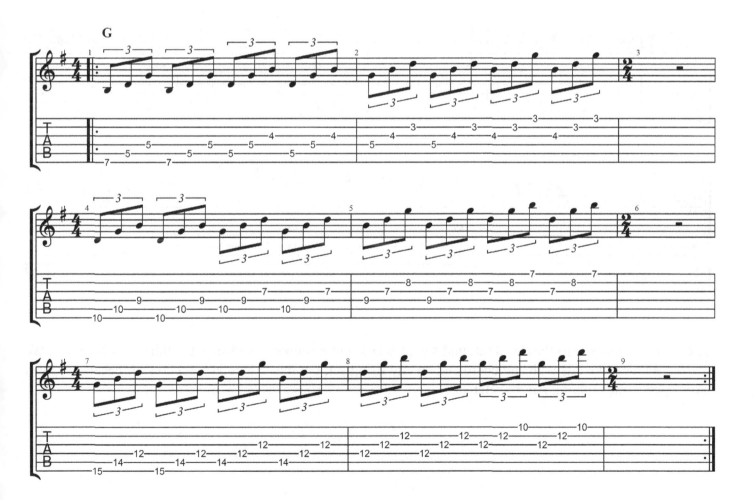

One of the hardest habits to break on the guitar is getting stuck in "the box", so we'll focus on that a little here.

When you've been used to playing scales in positions, it can be overwhelming to see a scale diagram that covers the whole neck, but our three-position chord system is going to give us specific areas of the fretboard we can target when moving up or down the neck.

In the next example, we're going to use double-stops to move from an A7 chord in the open position (A shape) up to the E shape. We start with the root and 3rd of A7 on the third/second strings, then ascend diatonically (raising each note a scale tone each time). A and C# become B and D, then C# and E, and we're into the E shape.

Next, we're aiming for the C shape. We can continue the pattern of 3rds on the third/second strings all the way up to the A shape and back down again.

Your goal here is to visualise the chord positions and think about how one position connects to the next. The more you practice connecting positions with ideas like this, the more you'll begin to intuitively connect other chords.

After doing it on an A7 in bars 1-4, repeat it for E7 in bars 5-8. Notice that the patterns that connect the positions are always the same.

Example 7b:

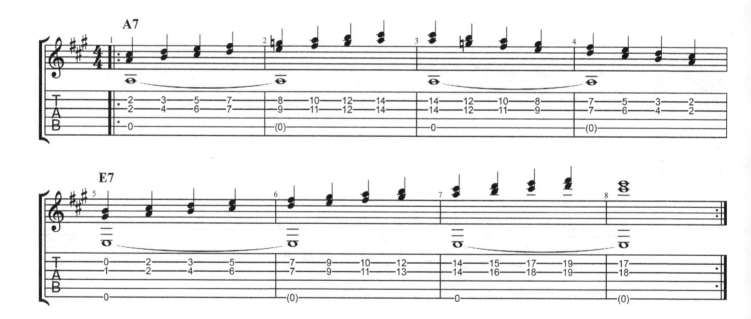

The next example swaps the chords around and plays the same connecting idea on the third/fourth strings. We can use an idea like this with any chord and on any string set, but this is a good place to start because we can have open strings ringing out for reference.

Example 7c:

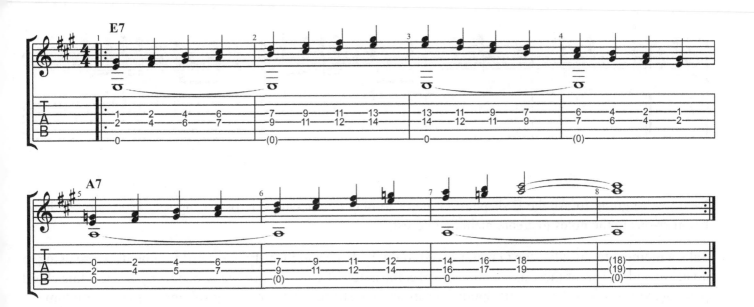

Here's an example of how we can take this idea and create a rhythmic, musical part for a song. Here we have 3rds as double-stops on the second/third strings. We can use them to play a melody that would work wonderfully over a groove in E.

This is how I'd play rhythm to a song like *Lovely Day* by Bill Withers.

Example 7d:

As well as double-stops, we can use the triad forms we learned to move between positions. If we play a G major triad in the E shape on the top strings, we can move up and play a G major triad in the C shape. To connect these shapes, we might play an A minor triad (chord ii in the key of G Major) in between them.

In bars 1-2, play the basic pattern holding onto the chords, then in bars 3-4 add some rhythm.

If you want an extra challenge, try reading and counting this rhythm before listening to it.

Example 7e:

Next, we're going to use the E shape of G major to play double-stops across string sets. Here we're adding hammer-ons to the notes to create melodic interest.

Take a moment to visualise the G major chord in the E shape and identify the chord fragments we're using to create this idea. I want these associations to become automatic for you, so that whenever you view this chord position, you know these melodic options lie around the shape, whether you're soloing or playing rhythm.

Example 7f:

Now, let's repeat this idea in the C shape.

These aren't the only options, of course, but these little chordal embellishments are a good place to start.

Example 7g:

Finally, here's the same concept again, moved up to the A shape.

When you're confident with these three positions, try this idea with some different chords, so you're set to play over anything you might need to.

Example 7h:

Now we're going to apply this idea to a tune to create some musical riffs. This example is inspired by the Sam and Dave classic, *Soothe Me*.

The only idea in this riff that you haven't already played is the chromatic approach. Look at the last double-stop in the first bar. These two notes (G# and C) aren't in the key, they are a half step below the next chord in the progression. Sliding into a chord from a half step below (or above) is always going to sound great!

Example 7i:

Here's another example, this time played to the chord progression of Marvin Gaye's *Let's Get It On*. Notice that we're using things we already know but plugging them into a different chord progression. The more we do this, the easier it's going to be to do it on the fly, on any chord progression.

Example 7j:

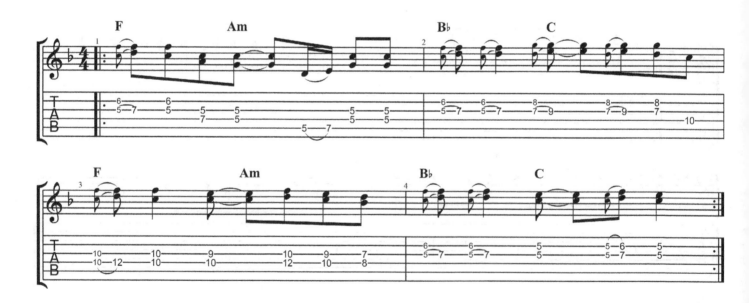

Let's finish up by digging a little deeper into the idea of chromatic passing notes with some vocabulary I took from great country players like Brent Mason, Johnny Hiland, and Scotty Anderson.

The following example moves from an open E chord up to the A shape with some chromatic passing tones to connect double-stops of the same shape. Think of it as a fill-in-the-blanks approach.

Example 7k:

Here's the same lick moved to an A major chord, moving from the open A position up to the C shape. We fill in the blanks between the two shapes with chromatic passing tones.

Example 7l:

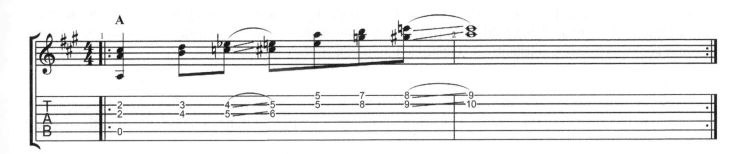

There's only so much we can cover of a genre in a single chapter. I could devote an entire book to soul or country music. In fact, as some of my long-time readers will know, I've already written multiple books on country music. Maybe books on soul will come next!

The idea here is to dip our toes into the water and find the things that excite us, so we can correct our course and focus on the things that interest us. The goal of practice is to take us towards who we really want to be as players.

See you in a week!

Routine Eight – 6ths and 7ths

Last week we looked into chordal work and applied it to real life music as a break from technique, but today we're going to delve a little further into the world of fretboard skills and picking technique by expanding on the diatonic interval exercises.

While I find 4ths pretty usable, and 5ths a little on the fringe, they both pale in comparison to the musicality of diatonic 6ths. These can be used to great effect in both single note work, and to provide melodic content for your rhythm work. They're used prominently in blues, soul, rock, jazz, country, and many more styles.

I see 7ths as being similar to 5ths. They are not hugely common in the work of well known guitar players (though John Scofield is a BIG fan!) and can sound a little jarring. But that doesn't mean you can't use them in your playing, and even if you don't, playing them creates a wonderful technical challenge for both fretting and picking hands. I remember working on these for hours in music school, and while they've not been a big part of my playing since, I don't regret spending that time. They really put to the test my ability to visualise a scale shape.

There may come a point with these exercises where you feel like you're trying to store endless new information and you're at breaking point, but I want you to really consider what we're doing here. We're not learning something *new*, we're applying a different pattern to a scale shape you already know. We're playing the same scale shape we've drilled constantly, but approaching it in a slightly different way.

We'll start the routine with a warm-up and play diatonic 4ths of the A Dominant scale from Routine Six, but with a slight twist. Rather than staying in the E shape, we're going to ascend the E shape, then move up to the C shape via the second/first strings. Then we'll descend the C shape and transition back down to the E shape at the bottom.

In theory you could make a transition point anywhere within these shapes, but the top and bottom are good places to start.

Example 8a:

Diatonic 6ths

Now let's look at diatonic 6ths. With their wider interval, there is enough distance between the notes to make 6ths sound very fresh, compared to smaller intervals like 3rds.

It's important to note that 6ths are just inversions of 3rds. The distance between the notes C and E is a third, but the distance between E and C is a 6th. It's the same notes flipped around. Because of this, 6ths have a similar melodic quality to 3rds, but the way they are arranged on the guitar gives them a different effect.

First, we'll work on 6ths by playing them in an ascending pattern, using the A Dominant scale we've been drilling.

Example 8b:

Now let's play the same thing in a descending pattern.

Example 8c:

We could work with these patterns further and mix ascending/descending directions for interest, but we covered that idea when working with 4ths and 5ths, so you know how to do that. I encourage you to work out those patterns for yourself and practice them.

Instead, we're going to change from playing 6ths as melodic events (one note at a time) to harmonic events (both notes sounding together).

When it comes to playing 6ths simultaneously, we have picking options. We can play them fingerstyle with thumb and finger, we can strum them (making sure to carefully mute the string in between), or we can hybrid pick them.

My preference is hybrid (I cover this technique in depth in my book *Hybrid Picking Guitar Technique* for those who want to explore it). I hold the pick between thumb and first finger and pick the lower note, and pluck the higher note with the second finger. Play the example in whatever way feels most comfortable to you.

Example 8d:

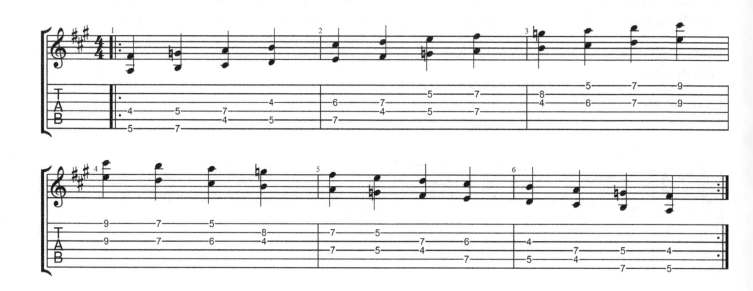

With the E shape out of the way, it's time to move up and look at the C shape.

I've waited until this point to draw attention to the modal benefits the guitar offers. So far, this shape has been played over an A7 chord, and we've viewed it and heard it as the A Dominant scale. Look at it closely, however, and you'll see that it has the exact same pattern as the D Major scale.

How so? Well, A7 is chord V in the key of D Major, and the A Dominant scale is like playing a D Major scale, beginning and ending on the note A.

It's still better to view the A Dominant scale as a *sound* in its own right that works over an A7 chord, but in terms of training your muscle memory, you're subconsciously working on two things at once, and could play these ideas over a D major chord.

Example 8e:

Finally, here are 6ths played in the A shape. If you're a CAGED player, you might recognise this as a D shape D Major scale. Again, it's all about building muscle memory and nothing will train that better than playing scales in intervallic patterns like this.

Example 8f:

Diatonic 7ths

Now we're going to explore diatonic 7ths. These are the widest intervals we're going to play, and they are both physically demanding on the picking/fretting hands, and challenging on the ear!

You may love these, or they may fall into the category of taking your medicine (like the 1234 chromatic workouts).

Example 8g:

Now let's play that descending. When working on this, focus on the picking motion. Pick down on the high E, and up on the G. This is a great example of inside picking – something we can always be better at.

Example 8h:

Now let's play diatonic 7ths harmonically in the E shape. I quite enjoy how these sound in the higher register – they can add a lot of spice to a solo!

Example 8i:

Next, we'll play through those same intervals up in the C shape.

Example 8j:

And finally (whew!) in the A shape.

Example 8k:

I don't want to leave you on the dissonant 7ths sound, so let's return to playing 6ths over an A chord. This time we'll move them across the neck, rather than remaining in position.

As we found in the last routine, this can be a great way to transition between positions, and there's a nice consistency when playing these intervals without changing strings.

First, let's do that on the third and first strings.

Example 8l:

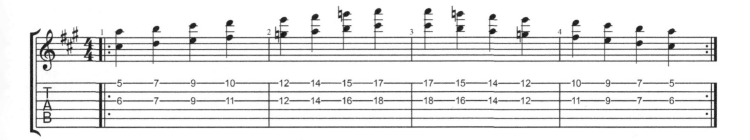

Now let's do that on the fourth and second strings. When playing this, don't forget to visualise the E, C, and A barre chord shapes that these intervals come from.

Example 8m:

Finally, here's the same idea, but on the fifth and third strings. I love using these when playing riffs in blues and soul music.

Example 8n:

That's it for this routine. I want to say that you're free of those hellish 7ths, but the reality is they'll always be a good exercise to keep your fretting/picking hand dexterity sharp, so don't be afraid to work them into your routines every now and again. They certainly can't hurt your playing!

Good luck, and I'll see you in a week.

Routine Nine – Articulation & Swing Picking

So far, we've devoted all of our attention to *what* we play: note choice, phrasing, rhythm, etc. Of course, this is essential work, because if we don't know what to play, we'll sit in silence! The problem is, while focusing on the *what,* it's very easy to lose sight of *how* we play.

Articulation is all about how we play our notes and it's incredibly important. How you articulate what you play will set you apart from musicians who, while technically proficient, can sometimes sound like a computer interpreting information on the page.

When I load a transcription into Guitar Pro and press play, the sound engine plays back the notes with uniform velocity and length. Real players don't do that, there is dynamic variation. Some notes are connected smoothly (legato) and some are detached (staccato), and this is what makes music interesting. Articulation is something we will gain incredible benefit from working on.

In the first book in this series we touched on legato technique, but in a way that focused purely on legato playing. Playing everything legato is no better than picking everything, so in this routine we're going to focus on a technique I call *swing picking*, which combines picking and legato skills and blends them into one fluid sound to emphasise a dynamic swing in our playing.

Picked notes are always going to sound louder than notes from hammer-ons and pull-offs. This means that, if we pick notes on the strong beats of the bar (beats 1, 2, 3 or 4), and hammer onto weak beats (the "&" of beats 1, 2, 3, 4), we'll put a dynamic accent on the beat. If we pick the weak beats and slur the strong beats, we'll create a dynamic accent off the beat. The latter approach creates a really musical sense of forward motion akin to that found in swing rhythms.

I love this technique. I love the sound and I love the way it feels. Plus, I love that it ends up making string crossing easier in most places. I've been teaching this technique for a long time and it's consistently a real point of frustration for students! I remember it being a huge struggle for me when my teacher first introduced it to me, but I pushed through.

It should be easy, but you've probably spent years training yourself to pick notes with downstrokes on the down beats. Now you're going to move the picking hand down, not pick a note, and instead play an upstroke on a weak beat?! That's going to be hard to do at first, but I promise, the time will be worth it.

Before we get into it, we'll start this week's routine with a review, playing diatonic 6ths on an A7 chord, starting in the E shape, transitioning up to the C shape, and then back down.

I'm opting to do my position shifting on the fourth and second strings, but you could work on doing it on the fifth and third, or third and first strings.

Example 9a:

Now let's move on to some basic swing picking exercises.

First, we're going to look at a four-note mechanic that has a *pick, pick, slur, pick* motion (where the "slur" part represents either a pull-off or a hammer-on).

The important part here is the picking motion. It must always be,

Down, up, (down), up

And NEVER

Down, up, (wait) down.

So, in this first example, it's incredibly important that as we pull-off from the 7th fret to the 5th, the pick continues down without picking, so that we are set up to play the next note (second string, 8th fret) with an upstroke.

Focus on the picking and play through this repeating four-note motif.

Example 9b:

Once you've got this under control, let's add two more notes to turn this idea into a six-note motif. This will help us to move beyond just playing four-note ideas that start on beats 1 or 3.

We'll play the six-note motif twice, leaving a pause between each repetition. Then we'll play it again without the pause. With the pause removed, notice that you're now slurring across the bar line, which sounds great!

Example 9c:

Next, we'll develop this six-note motif further and move it through a scale position. This time, every time you play the motif you'll move over to a new string set before ending on the D root note. Make sure you don't lose sight of the swing picking technique as indicated in the TAB below!

Build up speed on this idea over time. It'll feel incredibly awkward to get the picking right first time through. But when the picking mechanic becomes automatic for you, the speed will come easily. This makes sense because we are playing pull-offs before string changes, which gives the picking hand a little more time to accurately pick the correct string.

Example 9d:

Now we're going to listen to the difference this articulation trick can add to even a simple scale.

Here, we first of all play an A Dominant scale ascending from the root, picking each note. Then we play the same thing again, but now with swing picked articulation. The latter is always the same: slurs always come after upstrokes, because upstrokes are always on the weak beats.

Example 9e:

Now let's look at the exact same idea, but in a descending direction.

If you want to start making these lines really pop, try adding more of an accent to the upstrokes before the pull-offs. This will emphasise the weak beat accent and create an even better sense of dynamic swing.

Example 9f:

Next, let's look at one of my favourite exercises: combining arpeggios and scales.

In this exercise you'll ascend a four-note arpeggio and descend four scale notes. This is a great way of spelling out the harmony, as four out of four arpeggio notes are in the chord, and four out of seven notes in the scale are in the chord!

Notice the use of swing picking here, placed to emphasise that accent on a weak beat.

Example 9g:

In the previous example we left two beats of space between each group of eight notes. Now we'll remove that rest to create a longer, more flowing exercise.

I might not play this full, four-bar line when soloing, but I use bits of it all the time!

Example 9h:

Now let's take this idea and transpose it to work over a D7 chord, played in the A shape. After three bars we run out of space and can't keep ascending, so instead we descend the D dominant scale with swing picking to bring us back to the starting position.

Example 9i:

Now let's do the same over an E7 chord in the C shape. As with the A shape, there's not enough space in this position to ascend for four bars, so we ascend for two bars then descend the scale to get back to the root note.

Example 9j:

To get a feel for how this idea can be applied to real world playing, here's a musical line that works over an A7 chord. It begins in the C shape with a four-up-four-down pattern, before using some swing picking to move down the scale and transition into the E shape.

There are endless ways to do things like this, but this is a good one to get you started.

Example 9k:

We'll end this routine with another four-up-four-down musical idea, this time adding some chromatic approach notes to target the C# (3rd) of the A7 chord, which is always going to sound good in a blues influenced setting.

Example 9l:

This articulation trick is just the beginning, and it's going to take time to internalise it. To work on it, you could go back through previous routines and see if you can apply the *pick, pick, slur, pick* pattern to other exercises.

I'm certain it'll take a lot of work to become fluent at this, but you'll know you've learned the technique properly when you no longer need to prepare for it when playing, and you just do it.

Good luck and I'll see you in a week!

Routine Ten – Dorian Mode

You've put a lot of work in, but you've finally made it to week ten! Unlike school, today won't be about taking it easy, playing games and eating cakes! We're just going to keep working and look at a new scale, so that you'll be well equipped to play over minor 7 chords.

We've got two chords covered already. Over major chords we can play the major scale, and over dominant 7 chords we can play the dominant scale. So, what can we play over minor 7 chords?

There are two common choices for minor 7 chords: the Aeolian mode (otherwise known as the natural minor scale) and the Dorian mode.

Seeing as though we're at the end of the book, it seems reasonable to tease what's coming next: modes!

Derivative modal theory

There are two ways of explaining/teaching modal scales. The first, *derivative modal theory*, is where we draw a set of modes from the same parent major scale.

Let's use C Major as an example to explain this.

The C Major scale has the notes C D E F G A B

When we play this scale over a C major chord, it sounds like a C Major scale. The C note sounds like the root note, the E note sounds like the 3rd, the A note sounds like the 6th, and so on.

But if we play this scale over a G7 chord, it doesn't sound like a C Major scale anymore, because C is no longer the root note, it's the 4th. E isn't the 3rd anymore, it's the 6th. And the A doesn't sound like the 6th, it sounds like the 2nd.

In effect, we're now playing the G dominant scale (aka the G Mixolydian mode), the fifth mode of the C Major scale.

According to this way of thinking, the A Aeolian scale is the 6th mode of the major scale and has these notes:

A B C D E F G A

And the D Dorian scale is the 2nd mode of C Major and has these notes:

D E F G A B C D

Can you see the difference between those two scales?

Other than the fact that they have different starting points, they are the exact same set of notes. Therein lies the problem with derivative modal thinking. It's why I prefer *parallel modal theory*, and I believe you'll have more success with the latter approach.

Parallel modal theory

Parallel modal theory builds modes from a common root note. Without realising it, you've already done that in this book. Remember that we took the major scale and lowered its 7th degree by a half step to create the dominant scale?

The C Major scale (C D E F G A B, formula 1 2 3 4 5 6 7)

Became…

The C Dominant scale (C D E F G A Bb, formula 1 2 3 4 5 6 b7)

These scales are easier to compare, right? It's very clear to see that the dominant scale is just a major scale with a flattened 7th.

Let's compare another scale.

The C Dorian mode has the notes C D Eb F G A Bb.

In other words, it's like the C Dominant scale but with a b3.

C Dorian has the formula 1 2 b3 4 5 6 b7.

What about the natural minor scale?

C Aeolian has the notes C D Eb F G Ab Bb.

In other words, it's like C Dorian, but with a b6.

C Aeolian has the formula 1 2 b3 4 5 b6 b7.

Dorian and Aeolian are both minor scales, but they differ in one key way: the natural 6th of the Dorian gives it a brighter sound, while the b6 of the Aeolian creates a darker, moodier sound.

In the exercises that follow we'll dig into the sound of the Dorian scale and touch briefly on the Aeolian, but first we'll warm up with a review of swing picking. Let's ascend an A7 arpeggio, then come back down the dominant scale with a swing picking pattern. Loop around this several times to get the hands warmed up.

Example 10a:

Now let's familiarise ourselves with the Dorian mode. We'll do that by first playing through the A Dominant scale. Then we'll play it again, this time with a b3 (C instead of C#). That's Dorian. It's as simple as that, and you've already thoroughly drilled the dominant scale shape.

I've written this exercise ascending, with every note picked, but remember we can go up, down, pick every note, play it legato, or swing pick it. The sky's the limit.

Example 10b:

To get familiar with the Dorian sound in this scale position, let's apply a fours sequence and play it ascending and descending.

Example 10c:

The next example is based around the same scale position, but we're applying a diatonic 3rds sequence. I don't want to horrify you, but we could go through this again applying 4th intervals, 5ths, 6ths, even 7ths! However, I'm sure you don't want this routine to be 30 minutes long, so I've refrained from making you do it. By now though, you know how to do this, so instead I'm putting my faith in your desire to get better.

Example 10d:

With the scale pattern in place, let's apply our earlier four-up-four-down pattern. Here you'll ascend a four-note Am7 arpeggio and descend four notes of the A Dorian scale.

I've always found this approach an effective way of learning to hear how a mode/scale sounds, as well as how to visualise it around a chord.

Example 10e:

As with all of our other sounds, we need to be able to play these ideas anywhere we might need them, so here's A Dorian up in the C shape. Remember, there's only one note different between this and the A Dominant scale you already know. The focus here is learning where that one note (the b3) lives.

Example 10f:

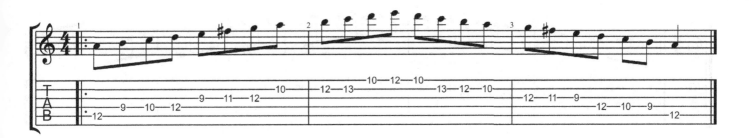

When you know this pattern well, applying a fours pattern to it shouldn't be too much of a bother. See what happens if you try to switch off your mind when you play this. Has it become automatic yet? If not, don't worry, it will.

Example 10g:

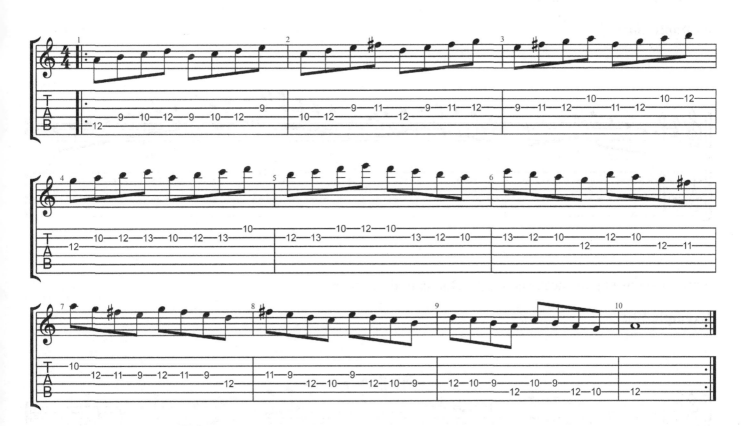

Let's try playing A Dorian in the C shape in diatonic 3rds. At this stage, hopefully this too should be automatic.

Example 10h:

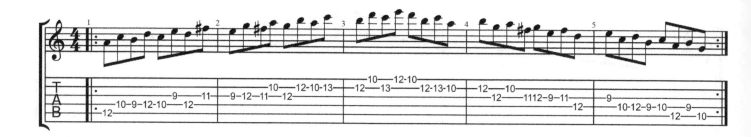

How about our four-up-four-down arpeggio/scale pattern, played in the C shape? When we run out of range, we can just come down the scale.

To mix things up a little, I've articulated this with swing picking. If you're not finding this hard, go back and practice swing picking the earlier exercises. Ask yourself which sound you like the best. Ignore what's hardest for you, just focus on sound.

Example 10i:

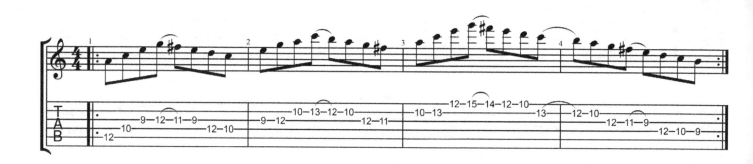

Now let's move up the neck and play A Dorian in the A shape.

Example 10j:

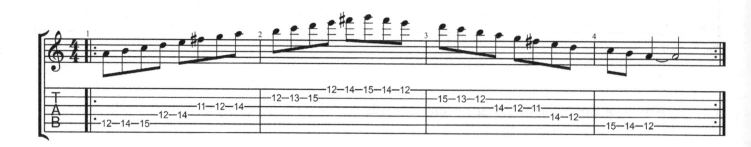

Now using our sequence of fours.

Example 10k:

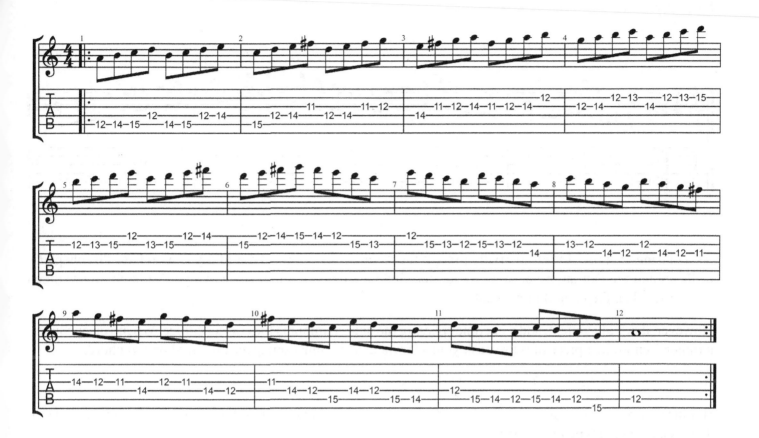

And now with diatonic 3rds.

Example 10l:

And, finally, four-up-four-down with the arpeggio/scale pattern.

Example 10m:

As a closing exercise, I want to briefly present the Aeolian scale. I went out of my way to base this chapter's drills around the Dorian, because it's a bluesier, funkier sounding minor scale that you're likely to use much more often than the natural minor scale.

However, that's all context, and sometimes playing the natural minor is the correct choice. When you encounter a minor 7 chord in a piece of music, ask yourself whether it's functioning as a ii chord or a vi chord.

In the progression Am7 – D7 – Gmaj7, Am7 is the ii chord in this ii V I sequence in the key of G Major.

But in the progression Am7 – F – G – Am7, Am7 is the vi chord in this vi IV V sequence in the key of C Major. This is an Aeolian type progression.

To show the huge difference in sound, here's me playing the A Aeolian (natural minor) scale in three positions over that progression. Much better than Dorian!

Example 10n:

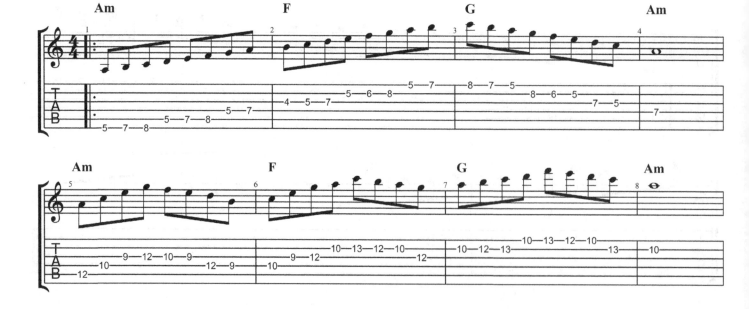

And you made it! The routine was a little longer this week, but hopefully it has given you plenty to mull over as you continue your journey of practice.

How well do you *know* the natural minor scale, for instance? We barely touched on it here, but I know you're now armed with enough knowledge on how to practice to work on it. You know exactly what to do to take this scale and solidify it, so get to work and I'll see you when you're ready for more!

Conclusion

Whew! You're finally at the end, although I think you understand this is just the beginning. I've always thought of music as a journey to a place you can see in the distance, and you just keep moving towards it. The problem is, the closer you get, the more is revealed just over the horizon, and those of us with curious minds find ourselves constantly changing the destination as we learn more and are excited by the possibilities.

I picked up the guitar because I wanted to play power chords in a punk rock band. 20 years have gone by and I've not played anything remotely punk-like in 15 years. I've learned other instruments. I've learned to read. I've learned several styles of music. I've studied music at school. I've taught thousands of students and reached millions more with educational materials and YouTube videos. I've travelled the world playing different things, recording music, writing music… but still, every day is a new day, and I'm excited about what I'm going to learn during the next 20 years and where that will lead me…

The bottom line is, the route there is practice. I've just got to put in the time to be what I want to be.

Spend some time with this book and learn the content inside out. Try coming up with some of your own practice routines that focus mostly on your areas of weakness and be that player who's always getting better.

I'm going to close the book with a story and a quote. I've read this many times over the years and it always drives me to keep moving forward.

Many years ago, while being interviewed at the age of 95, the great cellist Pablo Casals was asked this question:

"Mr Casals, you are 95 and the greatest cellist that ever lived. Why do you still practice for six hours a day?"

Without hesitation, Casals responded,

"Because I think I'm making progress!"

I picked this example because Casals made similar remarks at several points during in his life. Not only was it something he really felt, but when asked the question, he knew exactly what to come back with. It's like he had spent a lifetime of practice doing it.

Now, go do some practice!